TO DAUGHTERS
OF NARCISSISTIC
MOTHERS

TO DAUGHTERS OF NARCISSISTIC MOTHERS

NOTES FOR SELF-CARE AND SELF-LOVE

DANU MORRIGAN

AUGSBURG BOOKS
MINNEAPOLIS

TO DAUGHTERS OF NARCISSISTIC MOTHERS
Notes for Self-Care and Self-Love

Originally published by Darton, Longman and Todd, London, UK
Copyright © 2012 Danu Morrigan

Cover image: Zikatuha / shutterstock
Cover design: Cindy Laun

Print ISBN: 978-1-5064-6214-1
eBook ISBN: 978-1-5064-6214-1

INTRODUCTION

To the unloved daughter,

There is so much that you should have heard from your mother: advice, support, compliments, validation, encouragement, and so much more. All the things you longed and deserved to hear, but never did.

These notes are what a loving mother would say. They're what you need and deserve to hear. They're designed to read as if they're from your own inner mother, the part of you who is your own wise mother to yourself. This wisdom and love is accessible to you through your quietness and attention, and these notes are from that place of healing and kindness.

In these notes I refer at times to your toxic mother. This is the one who birthed you or adopted you and, by doing so, made an implicit promise that she would love you and honor you, and who failed in that. This reference to a toxic mother is to distinguish her from your inner mother, who does love you and care for you.

You'll see that themes are repeated. This is intentional. You need to hear the positive message many times to replace the many years of negative messages.

Although these notes are for all daughters who were unloved because of a mother's abuse and toxicity, they came from my work exploring the specific dysfunction of narcissistic personality disorder

(NPD). For more information and resources on that, I invite you to visit my website www.daughtersofnarcissisticmothers.com.

With my very, very best wishes on your journey to self-care and self-love,

Danu Morrigan

HOW TO USE THIS BOOK

You can use this book however you want, of course. But here are a few suggestions:

1. Read from beginning to end, in as few or as many sittings as you want, and enjoy the impact of all the messages of love, support, and advice in one go.
2. Read from beginning to end, one note a day.
3. Open the book at random and read the note there.
4. Use the notes like oracle cards. Pick a number between 1 and 207 at random, and see what message is picked for you.
5. For each note you read, especially if you just read one at a time, you can do any or all of the following:
   a. Just enjoy it in the moment.
   b. Ponder its meaning and message throughout the day.
   c. Journal about it.

You can, of course, mix-and-match these suggestions as you please—for example, by reading the book start-to-finish first, and then going back and reading one note a day.

Going forward, journaling is an excellent way of communicating with your inner mother yourself, quite apart from this book. Try freewriting, which is where you write without stopping for a given period of time or a given number of pages. If all you can write is "I don't know what to write" over and over, that's okay. But that won't happen—not indefinitely, at least. After a while your brain will know what to say, and that's when the magic happens, with messages from your subconscious.

Try using this process to communicate with your inner mother. You can write a letter to her by using the freewriting method, and then write back from her in the same way. Or write it as a dialogue, letting both you and your inner mother take turns speaking.

Yes, this is all a trick. Yes, it's all you. But it's a way of accessing the powerful, compassionate, wise part of you, the part that is a good mother to yourself.

My daughter, know this:

You are a gift to this world. You truly are.

My daughter, know this:

I love you.

I love the bones and the breath and the heartbeat of you.

My daughter, know this:

The day you were born, I felt such joy and happiness, and have felt it ever since.

My daughter, know this:

Your every breath is a gift to me and fills me with joy.

My daughter, know this:

You deserve to be treated well, especially by yourself.

My daughter, know this:

All feelings are appropriate, both yours and others'.

For sure, all actions are not appropriate.

But don't let anyone—you, or anyone else—deny your feelings or your right to have them.

My daughter:

Could you love yourself? Nurture yourself?

Could you be the mother to your own self, since I cannot be there in person?

What would you do to nurture yourself? Could you write a list of ways?

And then do them?

My daughter, know this:

The problem is not that you're communicating wrong, that you're not explaining it right to your toxic mother.

The problem is that she does not want to understand, and therefore will never understand. She is making it her business not to understand, and she can do not-understanding a lot better/longer/harder than you can ever do explaining.

So, my daughter, why not let go of the feeling that if you just find the right words, or say them sincerely enough, she'll get it?

Why not free yourself from that trap?

My daughter, know this:

If you have tried, and tried, and *tried* to fix things with your mother, but it never works, and she never meets you halfway, then it's clear the problem is with her and not with you.

No matter what she tells you about it all being your fault, the problem is with her.

My daughter, I want to ask you this:

When you take a shower or wash your hair, could you do it lovingly? Not just efficiently, I mean. But to wash your own body the way you would wash a child you loved. Lovingly, gently, mindfully.

Do it for me, your inner mother, as I cannot do it physically myself. And know that when you do that, I am there in that moment loving you.

My daughter, know this: You are too hard on yourself. Be gentler.

Be kind to yourself.

My daughter:

Speak gently to yourself.

Even if you make mistakes, just acknowledge them and see how you can do better.

Don't berate yourself. Don't shame yourself.

You have had enough of that and you do not need more.

My daughter, know this:

I am proud of you. So proud. The way you keep going despite it all.
You are a hero.

You really are. Believe it.

My daughter:

I would love to see you learn to respect your feelings, to just allow them to be. To honor them for showing up and telling you what's going on for you.

They're not always right, of course. But they're always real.

My daughter:

Laugh often. Seek out reasons to laugh. It is so good for you. And the sound of your laughter gladdens my heart.

My daughter, know this:

Have you any idea how beautiful you are?

No matter what you might think, you are beautiful.

I see this, and I know.

17

My daughter:

I invite you to practice seeing the joy in small things. The bud of a flower, the laughter of an overheard child, the feeling of the sunshine on your skin.

These are all little joys that are my gifts to you.

My daughter, know this:

If you struggle to see any joy in life, you might well have depression.
If so, I urge you to get help for this. It's hard to even want to get
better, but it's so worth it. You deserve to be well.

My daughter:

Whenever you see a coin on the street, know that it means I am thinking of you.

My daughter, know this:

You are precious.

You are so, so precious.

You have such value, just for being you. Believe this.

My daughter, know this:

You are beautiful, so very, very beautiful.

Your beauty is in the curve of your smile and the sound of your laughter and the sheer reality of you.

That you are here in this world, is your beauty.

My daughter, know this:

You are far more intelligent than you give yourself credit for.

Or maybe I should say: than your toxic mother made you believe was true.

My daughter, I ask you this:

Make the hard decisions as often as you can. The higher decisions.

To walk away from the toxic relationship, to eat well, to care for yourself.

My daughter, know this:

Your victory over your toxic mother lies in refusing to treat yourself as she treated you.

That is how you win.

Truly, the best revenge is living well. Live well, my beautiful daughter.

My daughter, know this:

Whenever you smile, my heart fills with joy.

My daughter, know this:

Floss! (By which I mean: look after yourself properly in all ways. Flossing is just a metaphor for that.)

My daughter, know this:

Don't let people abuse you. You are worth so much more than that.

I know your toxic mother taught you differently, but I am telling you: she lied.

You are worth nothing less than the highest good.

My daughter, know this:

It's okay to feel your feelings. They're barometers of what's going on for you. I know it's hard to identify your emotions sometimes when you were taught not to, but with practice it will get easier.

My daughter:

I would love for you to know how brave and strong and mighty you are.

Claim it now.

My daughter:

Be your own best friend.

And I invite you to really think about that statement, not just say glibly, "Yeah, yeah, I will."

Instead, think of this: If you could be your own best friend, what would you do differently? How would you speak to yourself more gently?

Do that.

My daughter, know this:

Your body is much more beautiful than you know.

It carries you every day, and is your home.

Care for it daily, stand tall, and carry that body lovingly.

My daughter, know this:

There is nothing you could have done to make your toxic mother love you. It's not because of a lack in you, as you thought, but because of the major lack in her.

You did not fail. She did.

33

My daughter:

Try to consciously see the beauty in the world. There is so much beauty.

Yes, there is ugliness too, and pain, and I do not ask you to be in denial of that.

But be sure to see, and appreciate, the beauty.

My daughter, know this:

Despite what you might think, you are very creative. Take a moment to appreciate all the areas of your life where you are creative. Maybe ask someone you trust to help you identify this.

My daughter, know this:

You always have the right to say no. You don't even owe an explanation or apology for this. A courtesy explanation or apology is fine, of course, if the asker is genuine. But that's a favor you're doing them, not anything you owe them.

Perhaps make it a default to say, "I'll think about that and get back to you," to give yourself time to consider whether this request is right for you.

36

My daughter, know this:

You are far stronger than you know, much more powerful than you realize.

My daughter, know this:

I am in awe of how well you have survived your toxic upbringing. I know you don't feel you've done well, but that you are still standing at all, no matter how shakily, is to your absolute credit.

Own that. Be proud.

My daughter, know this:

You're awesome.

Wonderful.

Amazing.

I could keep going all day.

My daughter, know this:

Laughter is very important. Try to find the laughter.

My daughter, know this:

Be gentle with yourself. Make it an absolute discipline to *always* speak gently to yourself.

That's nonnegotiable.

My daughter, know this:

Don't be scared of emotions, even strong emotions. These emotions are your friends.

The fear of emotion is an emotion, right? And you're already feel-ing that, and surviving it. You will survive the other emotions too: the pain and hurt and others. It won't be comfortable, but it is absolutely doable.

My daughter:

Don't forget that all emotions are valid; you do not have to apologize for them. All actions, however, are not valid, including sharing your emotions inappropriately.

But appropriately limiting your actions does not mean you have to limit, or deny, your emotions. If you're angry or hurt or scared, then you are angry or hurt or scared, and you don't have to invalidate that.

My daughter, know this:

You have no obligation to forgive your toxic mother. You may choose to let the anger go, to accept what happened, to move on in peace. So, yes, if that's forgiveness, you might well do that.

But what she did was not okay, and you don't ever have to say it was.

My daughter, I ask you this:

Try to show up as an adult each and every time.

It's not easy. Sometimes your child-self wants to express herself in unhealthy actions. It's more than okay to *want* that. Just, if you can, do not give into that want. Allow your adult-self to take charge. Relationships and situations will work much better the more you can do that.

My daughter, allow yourself time to play, whatever play means for you. Dance? Painting? Cycling? It doesn't matter what it is, just as long as you do it. This is part of self-care. It is important.

Play.

My daughter:

Feel the fear; allow it to fully *be* in your awareness. And the hurt.
And the anger. And the pain. Emotions are designed to be felt fully
so they can move on. It takes practice, and it means you have to be
willing to be fully present. It's not easy, but you have proven you have
so much courage, my beautiful daughter, so I know you can do it.

My daughter, are you looking after your physical needs: hygiene, exercise, nutrition, medical care?

Do.

Try to monitor your internal talk, my beloved daughter.

Catch yourself being self-abusive, and stop it in the moment.

Replace it with the kind word.

My daughter, be kind and gentle to yourself.

Always.

50

My daughter, know this:

Don't be scared to put yourself first where appropriate.

It's okay to do that—it really is—no matter that you were taught differently.

51

My daughter, know this:

Remember that you are far, far stronger than you realize.

My daughter, know this:

You are so beautiful.

Maybe you can't feel it or see it when you look in the mirror, but I tell you only the truth: you are beautiful.

My wish for you is that you see it too.

My daughter, know this:

When you make a mistake, it's something wrong that you *did*, not something wrong that you *are*.

My daughter, know this:

You are not responsible for anybody else's happiness. Never think you are, no matter how much they try to tell you that you are.

You are not.

You are obligated to treat them ethically and that is all. If they don't like it, that is their problem, not yours.

My daughter, know this:

If an abusive or unloving person calls you selfish, that's a badge of honor. It means you're honoring your needs rather than their wants.

Consider it, I suggest, a huge victory.

My daughter, know this:

There are gifts for you in this journey.

Well, maybe not gifts. They are not given to you. They are hard earned.

But they're yours.

What are they? Strength? Wisdom? Resilience? What else?

I invite you to name them, to own them, to cherish them.

To applaud yourself for them.

57

My daughter:

Try to have patience when others say, "But she's your mother! Of course she *loves* you!"

They don't understand.

They are so lucky not to understand.

My daughter, know this:

You are entitled to ask for help from others.

You don't have to do it all alone, no matter what your toxic mother taught you.

My daughter, know this:

It is safe for you to smile.

You look so pretty when you smile. It lights up your face.

60

My daughter, know this:

If you ask for help from others, how they react will give you good information regarding the health of your relationship.

A "no" isn't necessarily unhealthy, as they are entitled to say no to a request. But note how they phrase their "no," and how often they say no, or how begrudgingly they say yes.

My daughter, know this:

Try to move your body every day. It's your home, your beautiful home, and you need to take care of it.

My daughter, know this:

When you exercise, you prove your love and care for yourself.

63

My daughter, know this:

It truly is not your job to fix others' problems, unless it's your dependent child, and even then, only appropriately.

My daughter, know this:

It's okay to put yourself first sometimes. Indeed, it's essential.

My daughter, know this:

It's important not to use negative "I am" statements, such as "I am stupid."

Say instead: "I did something stupid."

Or even more kindly, "I made a mistake."

My daughter, have I told you how amazing you are even when you are doing nothing more than eating ice cream or lounging on the sofa?

Or even both together! You are amazing!

My daughter, know this:

You might not have accomplished as much as you would like to have done, or as much as others have, but considering the odds against you, all that you have accomplished is a huge success.

Claim that, I urge you.

Be proud of yourself, as I am proud of you.

My daughter:

Every time you see anything yellow today, know that I am thinking of you.

Actually, that applies every day. And for every color.

But for today, just concentrate on yellow, and think of me when you see it, and know I am thinking of you.

69

My daughter, know this:

You can own your mistakes without beating yourself up over them.

My wish for you is that you do just that.

My daughter:

Try to aim for reciprocity in relationships. Make sure you're not giving more than you're getting. This is on average, of course. If a friend is going through a crisis, it'll be all about her: her taking and you giving. But she needs to give to you when needed too. It should all balance out over time.

My daughter:

Try to walk more confidently. Pretend you're an actress in a play, playing the role of a confident woman. Head high, shoulders back. Stride.

Your mind believes your body language, so this confidence can become your truth.

My daughter, know this:

You are entitled to your own boundaries, both literal and metaphorical.

Your home is your space, and your toxic mother may not invade it.

Also, your private life is just that—private—and she has no right to ask inappropriate questions, and you have no need to answer them.

My daughter, know this:

If one of you has to be upset, it doesn't have to be you.

This is another way of saying that you don't have to keep your toxic mother (or anyone) happy at huge cost to your own peace.

My daughter, know this:

You deserve all good things in life. You do.

You might not feel like that, but you do. Believe me in this.

My daughter:

It's not easy being the truth-teller, is it? Even if the only one you tell the truth to is yourself.

It can be painful. But it's empowering. And freeing.

My daughter, know this:

Your toxic mother will never love you.

I know this isn't easy to hear, but your freedom lies in accepting that fact.

It means you can stop pouring energy into a useless quest, and use that energy for your own life.

My daughter, know this:

Every time you do something nice for yourself, you are winning twice. Once, by the nice act, and twice by the message your subconscious receives that you are worth being treated well.

My daughter, know this:

I am so very, very proud of you.

In every moment, I am proud of you. Never forget that.

79

My daughter, know this:

When you feel real love, or real pride in someone else's success, know that you are living life in a true, real, and authentic way such as your toxic mother will never experience. It's like she's living in a world of black-and-white and you are living in full color.

80

My daughter:

By all means, feel compassion for your toxic mother, stuck in her shadowy sepia life, devoid of the joy of true human relationships.

However, know that feeling compassion doesn't mean you need to accept abuse.

My daughter, know this:

You can forgive your toxic mother from a safe distance, if you are inclined to forgive her at all. Forgiving someone for past abuse doesn't mean you need to accept more abuse in the future.

My daughter, know this:

You deserve some pampering, you know. A spa (even one you do for yourself, if necessary), a nice long bubble bath, a haircut—what would you like?

Could you arrange that for yourself? Would you?

My daughter, know this:

If someone compliments you, believe them. Most people are genuine, and most compliments are meant genuinely. Maybe you really *are* that wonderful something they told you.

(Actually—there's no maybe about it!)

My daughter, know this:

I am thinking of you today.

Of course, I think of you every day, but I wanted to specifically remind you of that today.

I'm thinking of you and sending you all my love and hugs.

My daughter, know this:

Whenever you treat yourself badly, you are continuing your toxic mother's toxic work.

Don't do that, I beg you.

My daughter, know this:

It's okay not to be perfect. It's okay to make mistakes.

I know your toxic mother told you—by either words or attitude—that you had to be perfect.

But she lied.

My daughter:

Try to show up as an adult, always.

My daughter:

Know that you do deserve love, my sweet girl. You do.

My daughter, know this:

You're living your life without a road map, making the best decisions you can with incomplete information. That's the human condition. Don't be so hard on yourself when you take a wrong turn sometimes.

My daughter:

Try to learn from events. Learn about yourself, about others, about life.

In this way you constantly play the game of life better.

My daughter, know this:

It's tough making good and healthy decisions for yourself, especially when it goes against your beliefs about your value.

I applaud you and honor you for making those good, healthy decisions anyway.

92

My daughter, know this:

You are not who she said you were. She was wrong about you, fully.

All that she said was a reflection of her own toxicity only.

My daughter, know this:

I see you, and I see your beauty and goodness and value.

My daughter, know this:

I see your flaws as well as your goodness. They're not that big, the flaws. And they don't mean you're less of a person.

Despite what she told you, you don't have to be perfect to be lovable.

My daughter, know this:

If and when you treat yourself well, in that moment you are telling your toxic mother: "I win. I reject your lies and your treatment of me."

There is power and healing in such a statement.

My daughter, know this:

I love you. Just sayin'.

My daughter, know this:

Maybe today try doing one thing that scares you.

Just one little thing. And see how the world doesn't end.

You are braver than you know.

My daughter:

Don't forget that I am only ever a thought away.

Whenever you need advice or comfort, think of me, and I am there for you.

My daughter, know this:

All normal people are sometimes scared too, and nervous, and unsure. They just hide it, as you do. Everybody is making it up as they go along. The only ones who never second-guess themselves are the toxic ones.

My daughter, know this:

When it seems that everyone else has all the answers and you have none, remember that you are judging yourself from the inside out, and everybody else from the outside in.

You're not comparing like with like.

My daughter, know this:

You are valuable.

You need to know this, and to live it.

102

My daughter, know this:

The only way to win with your toxic mother is to stop playing.

Despite how it seems, nothing—*nothing*—obliges you to stay in that game.

My daughter, know this:

It's okay to honestly, calmly, and respectfully express your needs and wishes. How the listener reacts will tell you much about the health of your relationship with them. They don't have to agree with you, but they do have to listen properly to you.

My beautiful daughter:

I do hope you give yourself credit for all you're doing, no matter how little it seems.

It's all an achievement.

My daughter:

I remind you to do your personal care mindfully and gently. You are handling a precious thing: yourself.

My daughter, know this:

You survived a toxic, unloving mother; you can survive anything.

My daughter:

Dance.

Today, put on some music and dance. I will dance with you.

We can laugh at how clumsy we are, if we are. But we can enjoy it all the same.

My daughter, know this:

If criticism is about something you *do*, and is meant to improve your relationship with the person criticizing, try to listen to it calmly and see if there is merit in it.

If criticism is about who you *are*, then this person is not healthy for you.

My daughter, know this:

Sometime in the next twenty-four hours, you will see something special that is a message from me. You will know it when you see it. Take note of it, and let my message come to your mind. It'll be exactly what you need to hear in that moment.

110

My daughter, know this:

You are never ever, ever, ever, *ever* obligated to stay in the orbit of an abuser. It is your absolute right to remove yourself.

The fact that the abuser is a blood relative doesn't change that one bit.

111

My daughter, know this:

Your toxic mother taught you that you are grotesque and ugly and vile. It is not true. It was a lie that she told in order to control you.

It is not true, my beautiful daughter. Not true.

My daughter, know this:

You are clear and good and wonderful. Under the grime she layered relentlessly onto you shines the pure, sparkling diamond that you are.

Your job is to remove the grime and unearth the diamond that sparkles beneath—the diamond that is the real you.

113

My daughter, I tell you this:

Be compassionate with yourself, always.

My daughter, know this:

A healthy self-discipline is good—a kind, gentle, but firm discipline.

Self-bullying is not.

My daughter, know this:

Of course, it would not be right to proactively hurt your toxic mother.

Having said that, if she is hurt by the actions you take to protect yourself from her abuse, there is nothing to feel guilty about. She has truly brought that upon herself.

I read a great quote today from Bruce Lee, and I'd like to share it with you, my daughter.

It's this: "Don't fear failure . . . in great attempts it is glorious even to fail."

It's so true. The trying is the victory.

117

Allow yourself to be happy if you can, my daughter.

It's okay to be happy. It's safe to be happy.

118

My daughter:

I love the words of Søren Kierkegaard: "Life is not a problem to be solved, but a reality to be experienced."

You don't have to have all the answers immediately, or even soon, or even ever.

Just have fun and joy along the way, as best you can.

119

My daughter:

When there's a decision to be made, ask yourself what I, your loving mother, would advise, and listen within for the answer.

It will come to you.

Then, judge that answer on its own merits and make your decision. I do not seek to override your free will.

Don't be scared to live your life on your own terms, my darling daughter.

It's your life, after all.

Who else should get to dictate terms?

My daughter:

I know you might feel it's sad that you're only starting to heal now. All those wasted years, you might think. I ask you to consider how wonderful it is that you are on this journey now. Some unloved daughters never manage that.

Be proud of yourself and what you are doing.

My daughter, know this:

Your life is important—very important. But it doesn't have to be serious.

Try to laugh often.

My daughter, know this:

If you want to know what somebody is like, ask them to do a small favor for you. Their reaction will teach you a lot about who they are.

My daughter:

I love you *this* much:

Arms stretched as wide as they'll go

My daughter:

Don't forget to be kind to yourself. That's important.

That's essential, in fact. Nonnegotiable.

My daughter, know this:

You are never obligated to be the bigger person. Ever.

Healthy relationships have participants of equal size.

My daughter, know this:

If someone asks you to be the bigger person, think of what they're really saying. They're asking you to accept the other person's mistreatment of you.

They are thus not your friend in this instance, as they are enabling your abuser.

My daughter, know this:

Your journey is to reclaim yourself from your toxic mother's lies.

My strong wish for you is that you can find joy and freedom in that journey long before you reach the destination.

I think you will.

129

My daughter, know this:

It is so true that the best revenge is living well. Live well, my lovely, live well.

My daughter:

Whenever you can, get into nature, stand barefoot on grass, legs apart, sturdy, and feel yourself part of the planet on which you live.

You belong here.

131

My daughter:

Be a best friend to yourself.

You deserve such a good best friend.

132

My daughter:

If you are distancing yourself from your toxic mother in order to keep yourself safe from her abuse, you may feel guilt.

Know this: This guilt is not true. It's real, of course. This is not to invalidate you. But it's not true.

It's based on the belief that removing yourself from the clutches of an abuser is wrong.

That belief is, itself, wrong.

My daughter, know this:

If you have undeserved guilt, acknowledge it and feel it.

Thank it for showing up—it is your friend, trying to help you. It just has false information, the wrong information you were given in the past.

Tell it so. Say: "Thank you for being here and trying to help me, Guilt, but there is no need for you. I am not doing anything wrong."

134

My daughter, know this:

You do not have to protect your toxic mother from the consequences of her actions. She's an adult; she's responsible for the results of her actions just as we all are.

It is absolutely not your job to protect her from that, especially when it costs you so much.

135

My daughter:

Don't abuse your body as you might well be prone to do.

Treat it well and kindly, as a loving mother would.

Be your own kind mother to yourself in this way.

My daughter:

I invite you to take your hands and caress your face and imagine that it is me doing it, just as I would if I could be there. Focus on the being-touched more than the touching.

My daughter, know this:

Your toxic mother taught you that you had to be perfect to be loved.

It was a lie.

It's not true.

You're not perfect.

You never will be perfect, *and that's okay.* You are lovable anyway.

My daughter, know this:

I love you.

Did I tell you that recently? I should tell you more.

I will.

I love you.

My daughter, know this:

I love you.

I love the sound of your laughter and the curve of your quiet half-smile.

My daughter, know this:

I love you.

I love the strength of your shoulders and the abundance of your courage and the beat of your heart.

141

My daughter, know this:

I love you.

I love the kindness of your heart and the tenacity of your courage.

My daughter, know this:

I love you.

Just because you are you. I need no other reason.

My daughter, know this:

You are enough.

You are always and forever enough.

My daughter, do this:

Breathe.

Remember to breathe.

My daughter, know this:

Whenever you smile, I smile too.

146

My daughter, know this:

You don't have to do anything to impress me.

Just by being in the world, by living, you get an infinity of my love and approval.

My daughter, know this:

Your joy makes me so happy for you. I rejoice in your successes.

I laugh with your laughter.

148

My daughter, know this:

Next time it's possible for you, smell a flower and think of me and how much I love you.

My daughter:

What is your dream?

Do you dare to look at it again?

I know your toxic mother stole it from you. Can you reclaim it?

I want that for you.

My daughter:

They say, "What would you do if you couldn't fail?"

I invite you to look at it differently: What would you do if failure didn't matter?

Because the truth is that it doesn't.

Oh, I know we put feelings and emotions and baggage on failure, and it seems like it matters. But when you strip them away, failure doesn't matter.

Failure is, paradoxically, victory.

Failure means you tried, you had courage, you valued yourself enough to follow your dreams.

The only true failure, my daughter, is not trying.

151

May I suggest, my daughter, that you give yourself massive credit for all that you have achieved, against all the odds? It hasn't been easy—any of it—and you deserve the credit for it all.

I applaud you.

I hope you applaud yourself.

My daughter:

Don't take over your toxic mother's job for her.

You know, the job of running you down and belittling you and not caring for you. That job.

If you have taken it on, then resign. Don't even give any notice.

My daughter:

Don't ever expect your toxic mother to change. She won't.

If she could have, or wanted to, she would have done so already.

Freedom comes from accepting this truth—truly, deeply, totally accepting it.

154

My daughter, know this:

It's okay to be selfish. Sure, not to the detriment of others, as toxic people are.

But to value your own wants and needs and to make them a priority—that is very okay.

More than okay: essential.

What treat could you give yourself today, my daughter?

Will you do it?

I'd love it if you would. You so deserve it.

156

My daughter, know this:

I love you.

I'm thinking of you.

I send you all the hugs.

My daughter, know this:

Sometimes your deep beauty leaves me breathless.

The beauty of you being you.

Laugh often, my daughter. Laugh often.

My daughter:

Your joy makes me so happy, you know. Your successes gladden my heart.

I celebrate each and every one, no matter how small.

160

My daughter, know this:

There are days when I feel I could just burst with joy and happiness to have you as my daughter.

How did I get so lucky as to have *you*?

My daughter:

Don't forget to make time for fun for yourself. Play is so important.

So, play.

My daughter, know this:

It's essential to acknowledge when you have been at fault. This is part of being an adult and, therefore, being a healthy person who can create good relationships.

Your toxic mother could never do this, and look at the trouble that caused.

My daughter, know this:

It's okay to make mistakes; it really is. Mistakes are proof we're living, and trying, and creating. They're good things, in truth.

For sure, don't seek them out! But don't let a mistake knock your confidence.

My daughter, know this:

Some days, continuing to stand is success all by itself.

Claim that success too.

My daughter, know this:

You are fully entitled to have, and to enforce, boundaries.

And if someone doesn't like that, that is their problem.

My daughter, know this:

It is not your responsibility to make your toxic mother's life work for her. She's an adult, and unless she is legally unable to make her own decisions, she owns her own life and is responsible for it.

167

My daughter, know this:

Others will most likely judge you for removing yourself from your abusive, toxic mother (if that's what you choose to do). I urge you to let that be okay. You can't control what they think, so don't waste your energy even trying.

Never make life decisions (such as staying in touch with your abusive mother) based on others' opinions.

My daughter, know this:

You deserve to be respected, and you are fully within your rights to remove yourself from people who do not respect you.

169

My daughter, know this:

You belong here in this world, on this planet. I know it might not feel like it, but you do.

I know this.

My daughter, know this:

Try to smile even when you don't feel like it. Our bodies impact our mood as much as our mood impacts our bodies.

Yet, don't feel you have to smile to make others feel better.

This is about you doing what's right for you.

My daughter:

Could you get yourself a bracelet to wear all the time, and let that bracelet be your reminder that I love you always, that you deserve to be loved by you, and that you deserve to be treated well?

172

My daughter, know this:

Your toxic mother stole your past. Don't let her steal your future.

My daughter:

Dance.

As they say, dance like no one is watching. In fact, make sure no one is watching. Then dance with abandon.

It's so good for you, and I love you doing things that are good for you.

My daughter, know this:

I love you. I love you I love you I love you.

I love you. I love you.

Oh, and did I say—I love you.

My daughter, know this:

It doesn't matter what the rest of the world thinks of your decisions regarding contact with your toxic mother. I know it hurts if they judge you. But they don't know the truth about how bad she is. You deserve to be away from abusers even if that offends some people. Their opinion need not be your business. Their bad opinion of you is part of the price you pay for your freedom, and only you can decide if it's worth it.

My daughter, know this:

It's bad enough that your toxic mother abused you all those years, but how much worse it is for you to do it to yourself. I know the habit is there, but truly, the best gift you can give yourself is to release that habit.

Treat yourself well, always, like the precious being you are.

My daughter:

May I suggest that you start writing a list of all the good things about yourself, no matter how small? (But don't forget the big ones too!) As you go through your day, try to consciously collect examples of good things about you.

Ask supportive friends and family to help too, maybe.

My beloved daughter, know this:

Sometimes it* really is about you, and that's appropriate.

Claim that.

*The occasion, or the conversation.

My daughter, know this:

Watch carefully for "You are . . ." statements, either from yourself or from others. If those statements do not end with empowering and validating words, they are unhealthy. If someone has a complaint about you, they should complain about your actions, not about who you are.

My daughter, know this:

If someone exhausts you when you're in their company, that's a warning flag that they're not good for you. They might not be abusive or manipulative, but they're an energy vampire nonetheless.

181

My daughter:

You're still here. That's a win for you. And for the world.

182

My daughter, know this:

I love your smile.

My daughter, know this:

Baby steps are good, you know. We all started with baby steps, and look at us now. So don't run yourself down if that's all you can manage so far.

My daughter:

Could you learn to love the scars your toxic mother inflicted?

They're the legacy of the life you lived and of how much you have overcome.

They're part of you and, as such, are precious.

The laughter.

Don't forget the laughter, my daughter.

186

My daughter, know this:

Your toxic mother drew you a portrait of you that is grotesque and horrible, and you—understandably—believed it.

I am here to tell you that this portrait is not accurate. It was her projection, and nothing to do with you at all.

Your job is to learn to think of yourself as fine and wonderful and perfectly, reasonably, averagely flawed.

My daughter, know this:

It is fully appropriate that you feel anger for what was done to you.

The trick is to fully feel it, and allow it, and then let it go. It does not serve you to dwell in that anger, but neither does it serve you to deny it.

Don't forget: you're allowed to feel your emotions now.

My daughter, know this:

I love you.

Just because you are you.

You don't have to earn that love. It's already yours.

189

My daughter, know this:

Today I am sending you the biggest, strongest, most loving hugs.

Try to imagine them, and the feeling of being loved and cared for and celebrated, that I send with them.

My daughter, know this:

Don't be scared to close the door—both literally and metaphorically—to toxic people.

You deserve to have only good people in your life.

My daughter, know this:

Even healthy people in your life will be flawed and challenging at times—that's the nature of the human condition. And that's okay.

The trick to knowing if they're toxic is whether they respect you or not.

My daughter, know this:

I love you, my daughter. I am always thinking of you.

My daughter, know this:

I am your biggest fan.

Your cheerleader, even. I root for you always.

(Can you see the pom-poms?!)

194

My daughter, I ask you this:

Can you try to be more comfortable with uncertainty? I know control feels safe. But you can't control everything, and it's exhausting to try, isn't it?

If you can manage it, there is a kind of comfortable certainty in uncertainty.

My daughter:

Do your best, and do that fully.

But don't beat yourself up for not being able to do more.

My daughter, know this:

You were not the cause of your broken relationship with your toxic mother, and therefore, you cannot fix it.

I hope there is freedom for you in knowing you can stop trying.

My daughter, know this:

You do not have to earn your place in this world.

It's yours by right.

My daughter, know this:

It's okay to feel whatever you're feeling. Don't "should" yourself out of that.

What actions you take are a different thing. You need to take owner-ship and be an adult then.

But your feelings are fine.

My daughter, know this:

It's okay to feel sad when bad things happen, or about sad things that already happened.

You don't have to talk yourself out of that or feel it is inappropriate.

My daughter:

May I suggest you try to take the word *should* out of your vocabulary? With rare exceptions, it's a very disempowering word.

Use instead *could* or *choose*.

My daughter, know this:

Others should not tell you what decisions to make or what paths to follow.

They can offer suggestions, for sure, but not instructions. They're not the expert on your life.

My daughter:

You are infinitely precious. I know this.

My daughter, know this:

It's essential to keep relationships roughly equal regarding time, favors, regard, share of the conversation, and so on.

204

My daughter:

You always do your best. I know that.

205

My daughter:

Don't believe anything your toxic mother says about you. She does not have your best interests at heart, so any of her opinions about you are based on her agenda, not your well-being.

If she is right, it is only by accident, and how will you know when that is?

I am only ever a thought away from you; remember that, my precious daughter.

My daughter:

Be kind to yourself, always.

Sometimes that kindness manifests as self-discipline, and sometimes as self-indulgence.

But it is always for your highest good. And it is always gentle.

207

My daughter:

We have come to the end of these notes. But my journey with you is never-ending. I am always with you. And more importantly, *you* are always with you.

Be your own champion and support and loving mother.

I wish you adventures and fun and flowers and laughter and silliness and joy going forward.

Your inner mother